TOOLS FOR TEACHERS

- **ATOS:** 0.9
- **GRL:** B
- **LEXILE:** 140L
- **CURRICULUM CONNECTIONS:** community helpers
- **WORD COUNT:** 69

Skills to Teach

- **HIGH-FREQUENCY WORDS:** are, helps, of, they, us, who
- **CONTENT WORDS:** bus drivers, crossing guards, day care workers, doctors, families, fire fighters, lifeguards, nurses, police officers, safe, teachers
- **PUNCTUATION:** periods, question marks, exclamation point
- **WORD STUDY:** long /a/, spelled a_e (safe); r-controlled vowels (care, doctors, drivers, guards, lifeguards, nurses); long /i/, spelled igh (fighters); long /e/, spelled i (police); /s/, spelled c (police, officers)
- **TEXT TYPE:** information report

Before Reading Activities

- Read the title and give a simple statement of the main idea.
- Have students "walk" though the book and talk about what they see in the pictures.
- Introduce new vocabulary by having students predict the first letter and locate the word in the text.
- Discuss any unfamiliar concepts that are in the text.

After Reading Activities

Encourage children to talk about the different community helpers featured in the book. Have they ever met any of them? Does knowing these people help them feel safer?

Tadpole Books are published by Jump!, 5357 Penn Avenue South, Minneapolis, MN 55419, www.jumplibrary.com

Copyright ©2018 Jump. International copyright reserved in all countries. No part of this book may be reproduced in any form without written permission from the publisher.

Editor: Jenny Fretland VanVoorst **Designer:** Anna Peterson

Photo Credits: Dreamstime: Kevin Lohka, 12. Getty: Fuse, 4; Maskot, 5; Johner Images/Trangius, Lars, 8; Caiaimage/Martin Barraud, 14–15. iStock: kali9, 10. Shutterstock: Chad McDermott, cover; Tatiana Popova, cover; michaeljung, 1; Ermolaev Alexander, 2–3; XiXinXing, 6, 7; Michael Courtney, 6; Netfalls Remy Musser, 9; matka_Wariatka, 13. SuperStock: VWPics/age fotostock, 9; Onoky, 11.

Library of Congress Cataloging-in-Publication Data is available at www.loc.gov or upon request from the publisher.
ISBN: 978-1-62031-762-4 (hardcover)
ISBN: 978-1-62031-782-2 (paperback)
ISBN: 978-1-62496-609-5 (ebook)

WHO HELPS KEEP US SAFE?

by Erica Donner

TABLE OF CONTENTS

tadpole books

WHO HELPS KEEP US SAFE?

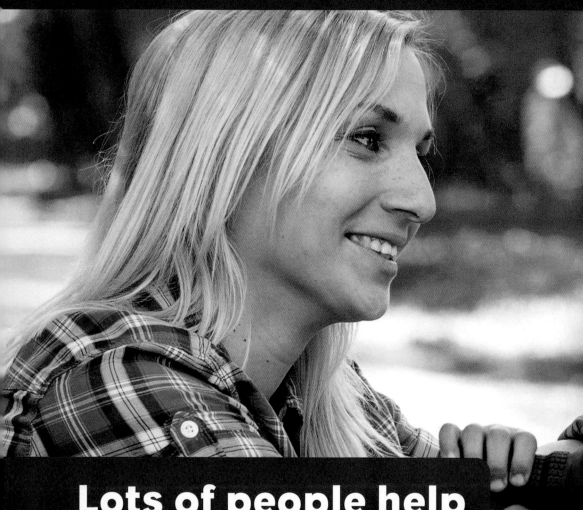

Lots of people help keep us safe.

Who are they?

Families keep us safe.

Doctors keep us safe.

Fire fighters keep us safe.

6

Police officers keep us safe.

teacher

Teachers keep us safe.

8

Lifeguards keep us safe.

Crossing guards keep us safe.

Nurses keep us safe.

Bus drivers keep us safe.

Day care workers keep us safe.

13

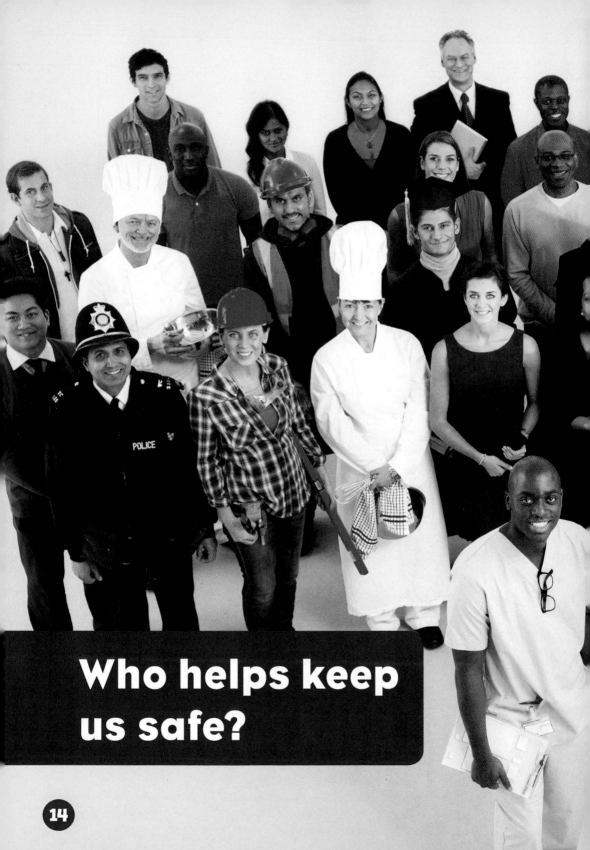

Who helps keep us safe?

Lots of people!

WORDS TO KNOW

day care worker

doctor

family

fire fighter

lifeguard

police officer

INDEX